WELCOME TO THE WORLD OF
Wolves

Diane Swanson

Whitecap Books
Vancouver / Toronto

The information in this book is true and complete to the best of our knowledge.
All recommendations are made without guarantee on the part of the author or
Whitecap Books Ltd. The author and publisher disclaim any liability in connection
with the use of this information. For additional information please contact
Whitecap Books Ltd., 351 Lynn Avenue, North Vancouver, BC V7J 2C4.

Edited by Elizabeth McLean
Cover design by Steve Penner
Cover photograph by Victoria Hurst/First Light
Interior design by Margaret Ng
Typeset by Margaret Ng
Photo credits: Robert Lankinen/First Light vi; Lynn M. Stone 2, 12, 22;
Thomas Kitchin/First Light 4, 16, 18, 24; Peter McLeod/First Light 6, 10,
14, 20, 26; Jeff Vanuga/First Light 8.

Printed and bound in Canada

Canadian Cataloguing in Publication Data

Swanson, Diane, 1944–
    Welcome to the world of wolves

    (Welcome to the world)
    Includes index.
    ISBN 1-55110-491-1

    1. Wolves—Juvenile literature. I. Title. II. Series.
QL737.C22S92 1996   j599.74'442   C96-910368-9

Contents

World of Difference   1

Where in the World   5

World of the Hunter   9

World of Words   13

New World   17

Small World   21

Fun World   25

Index   28

World of Difference

MEET A WONDER DOG:
THE TIMBER WOLF.

It's a dog with a difference. The wolf is a wild dog—big and strong. It's the biggest wild dog in the world.

Male wolves grow larger than females. A male can grow so tall, his shoulder stands higher than a kitchen table. A very big wolf can weigh as much as a man.

Wolves have bristly fur and bushy tails, but they don't all look alike. They come in different sizes and colors. Some are black and some are white. Others are

In winter, a white wolf blends with the snow. In summer, you can spot it from far away.

1

The rare red wolf of southeastern United States is smaller and lighter than most timber wolves.

tan, brown—even reddish. But most wolves are gray with streaks of other colors. That's why timber wolves are also called gray wolves.

Unlike many animals, wolves build close families. Parents and their young all live together in a pack of up to 20 or more. They travel together, feed together, play together, and sleep together. Sometimes, an aunt or uncle of the pups joins a pack.

Wolf families are loving and loyal. The parents usually stay together their whole adult lives. They help each other care for their family and keep it safe.

As young wolves grow, they help the parents look after newborn pups. Some of these young wolves stay with their family three or four years. Then they may leave to find a mate and start a new pack—a family of their own.

What a surprising animal is the wolf! Here are just some of its wonderful ways:

- A wolf can walk slippery logs—by spreading its toes.
- A wolf is a strong swimmer; it even chases beavers through water.
- A wolf can sniff out clues to learn which wolves— male or female—have been near its home and how long ago.
- A wolf will raise orphan pups—as well as its own family.

Where in the World

A wolf's home is enormous and wild.

DON'T LOOK FOR WOLVES IN TOWN. Most stay far away from people. These wild dogs make wild places—the wilderness—their home.

Some packs are forest wolves. They run among the shadows of the trees. Others are tundra wolves that race across the treeless northlands.

Each wolf pack has a home, a territory that the wolves claim as their own. Their home is huge. An especially huge territory can be much larger than a big city—even 5000 square kilometres (2000 square miles). Where there is

5

With a big yawn, this wolf is ready to flop down on the snow. Another in its family is already snoozing.

plenty of food, territories are smaller.

During fall, winter, and early spring, a pack tours its territory. The wolves often travel up to 32 kilometres (20 miles) a day. They hunt for food, tend their families, and keep the land free of other wolf packs.

Wolves mostly go about their business in the dim light of early morning and evening. When the sun is high—in the middle of the day—wolves usually lie down and sleep.

Many years ago, there were more wolves than there are now. And they lived in more places in the world.

Today, there are few wolves in Europe or the United States—except in the state of Alaska. But wolves still live all across Canada and in several parts of Asia.

HOW WOLVES CAME

When the northern lights danced, wolves came to visit. That's what some native North Americans believed. They saw the flashes of purple, red, and green light as signs of wolves bounding from sky to Earth.

Scientists think wolves developed from an ancient animal they call Mesocyon. It lived about 35 million years ago. The Mesocyon was a small "half-dog" with short legs and a long body. It may have lived in packs as wolves do.

7

World of the Hunter

Long legs and big feet help a wolf run through snow and brush.

FINDING FOOD FOR THE FAMILY KEEPS WOLVES VERY BUSY. Sometimes they nibble berries and bits of grass. But mainly, wolves need meat, so they are hunters.

Keen senses help wolves hunt. They can see as well as you can. They can smell a deer 2 kilometres (more than a mile) away. They can hear noises from even farther away than that.

Wolves are built to chase the animals they sense. They have long, strong legs and big feet. They can race up to 65 kilometres (40 miles) an hour and

9

This wolf is digging up an easy meal— food buried after an earlier hunt.

trot half a day without resting.

On its own, the wolf can catch animals smaller than itself: mice, squirrels, rabbits, and birds. But with its pack, the wolf can catch animals much bigger than itself: deer, moose, buffaloes, and musk-ox.

Wolves hunting in a pack often work as a team. They might take turns chasing their prey to tire it out. They might trap their prey by forming a circle around it. Half the pack might chase the prey toward the other half.

After a successful hunt, the wolves feed. They may bury some of the meat—food for days when hunting is poor. They also carry some back to pups too young to follow the hunt. In the world of the hunter, all the pack eats.

DINNER ON THE RUN

A wolf spots a mouse. The wolf sneaks forward. Its eyes are fixed; its muscles, tense. Slowly, softly, carefully, it creeps. It is all set to dash, but it hopes to move closer first.

Then the mouse spots the wolf. The mouse freezes. The wolf freezes, too.

Suddenly, the mouse bolts, and the wolf leaps after it.

In seconds, it's all over. Another dinner on the run.

World of Words

IT'S A GOOD THING WOLVES CAN TALK. That helps them live and hunt together. They whimper, bark, growl, and howl. They use their bodies to say things, too.

Howling is one way a pack warns another to stay out of its territory. Wind can carry these long, loud cries for more than 6 kilometres (about 4 miles).

Wolves in a pack also howl about hunting. They howl to get ready before a hunt. They howl to keep in touch while they hunt, and they howl to cheer after a hunt.

A pup asks for food by licking the nose and mouth of an older wolf.

13

Howling helps wolves in a forest find each other again.

When a wolf leaves a pack, it howls its goodbyes. Then it howls for a mate. If another wolf hears the howl, it answers. It may even answer people if they howl like wolves.

Growls and snarls make good threats. Bared teeth and wrinkled noses make even better ones. When one wolf threatens another, it also raises its ears and tail. It stares hard. It fluffs out its fur, raises its back, and straightens its legs. That way it looks bigger and taller than it really is.

The wolf that is threatened may close its mouth and flatten its ears. It may tuck its tail between its legs and lower its body. It may even roll over, tummy up, and flop its head right back. "You win. Let's not fight," it is saying—without making a sound.

PUT ON A HAPPY FACE

If you were a happy wolf, you would show it. And your whole pack would know it.

Your eyes would shine. Your ears would point forward. Your mouth would fall open, and your tongue would dangle out. You might be so happy you would leap and yip. Your whole body would wiggle with joy.

The happy sight might draw your mother close. You would see her tail wag and feel her tongue lick your nose. That's "I love you" in wolf talk.

15

New World

THE BIRTH OF PUPS MAKES SPRING SPECIAL. Before the big day, a mother wolf finds a place to have her pups. She looks for a den, shielded from wind and rain, and safe from danger. It may be a tunnel, a cave, a hollow log, or a cozy nook among thick shrubs.

The mother and her pack might make a new den. Or they might choose one that is well used. In the frozen north, wolves have used some of the same caves for hundreds of years.

When it's time to give birth, the whole pack gathers outside the den.

Cozy in their den, these three-week-old pups—of different colors—all have the same mother.

17

Caring for new pups is a full-time job for a mother wolf.

Throwing their heads back, the wolves howl a welcome to each pup. They lick one another and wag their tails to celebrate the births.

Up to 11 tiny pups may appear. Each one weighs only as much as a loaf of bread. The pups can't hear or see their new world yet, but their mother stays close to keep them safe. Milk and warmth flow from her body.

For about three weeks, the mother wolf lives in the den with her pups. Her mate and others in the pack bring food to her.

By the fourth week, the pups spend some time outside the den. If anything scares them, they pop back in. Another wolf may "babysit" the pups for a few hours. Finally, their mother can rest.

DEEP IN THE DEN

Few people enter wolf dens, but one man did. He crawled through a hole the size of a bed pillow. Then he crept through a narrow tunnel underground.

After crawling 2 metres (6 feet), he came to a smooth hollow. An adult wolf had slept there.

From that point, the tunnel turned sharply and sloped upward. The man followed it another 2 metres (6 feet). At the end was a second hollow—once a cradle for wolf pups.

Small World

HAWKS AND EAGLES SOAR OVER-HEAD. They are watching and waiting to snatch a wolf pup.

But the wolves are watching and waiting, too. They stand guard as the pups bob in and out of the den. And they keep up their guard when the pups—only two months old—leave the den for good.

As the pups sleep and eat with the other wolves, they become part of the pack. The pups and young wolves chase each other and play together. The young ones follow the older ones around.

At two months, a wolf pup is ready to start exploring its world. It may live for 13 years or more.

21

The small world of the pups grows as they do. The pack takes them farther from the den. The older wolves start to teach them the ways of the wild.

Wolves are strict teachers. They growl if the pups don't behave. They bite if the pups are really bad. Many times a

Besides drinking from lakes and streams, pups learn to sniff around them for signs of prey.

day, parent wolves knock over the pups and hold them down for a second. That's the wolf way of teaching who's boss.

By late fall, the pups can travel far. They can even follow their pack on hunting trips. They start to learn how huge their territory really is.

One by one, the pups walk in line behind the adults. When snow falls, the pups step right into the footprints the big wolves make. This makes traveling their world a little bit easier.

A wolf pack was sleeping. Suddenly, its leader jumped up and growled deeply. His mate repeated the growl.

Racing to the den, the mother wolf urged her pups to follow. Their father came behind, nipping a slow-moving pup. When everyone was inside, the parents lay at the opening.

Heavy footsteps pounded the ground overhead. But inside the den, all was quiet. There the pack stayed until their greatest enemy— people—had passed.

Fun World

A WOLF PUP LEAPS IN FRONT OF ANOTHER—front legs down, rear end up. Its tail wags furiously. "Let's play," it is saying. And the two pups tear off together.

Like children, wolf pups play a lot. They tumble, they wrestle, they pretend to fight. They often take turns chasing each other.

Pups play stick games. One pup grabs a twig and uses it to tease another wolf. That leads to a chase or a game of tug-of-war.

A wolf pup also plays alone. It rolls

Play is giving these young wolves a good run—exercise to keep them healthy.

Ravens tease wolves for fun and for food. Sometimes, they snatch meat from a surprised wolf.

over—and over and over. It chews sticks or chases its tail. It pounces on flowers or on leaves that flutter. Racing, leaping, it snaps at bees and butterflies.

Pups play hard, then take long, deep naps. As they grow, they race and chase for hours before they tire.

Play is not only fun. It helps pups develop. It teaches them to watch and listen—and to react fast. It exercises their muscles and helps the pups grow strong. It trains them to run fast and far. And it helps them learn how to fight and hunt.

Playing together makes pups feel closer to each other and to the adult wolves that play with them. It helps wolves learn to live and work together.

RAVEN TAG

Where there are wolves, there are often ravens. These big, black birds grab leftovers from wolf hunts. And just like wolves, they like to play.

Ravens play with each other. They slide down snowbanks, pass sticks—beak to beak—and turn somersaults in the air.

They also play by teasing wolves. Ravens dive at the wolves, then speed away. They peck the wolves' tails. They even play "catch-me-if-you-can" by getting the wolves to chase them.

27

Index

Alaska 7
Asia 7

Birds 10, 21, 26, 27
Birth 17–18

Canada 7
Color 1–2, 17

Dens 17, 19, 21, 22, 23

Europe 7

Families 2–3, 6, 9,
    17–19
Feeding 2, 9, 11, 19, 21
Food 6, 9–11, 19
Forests 5, 13

Gray wolves 2
Guarding 3, 19, 21, 23

Hearing 9, 18
Height 1, 15
Homes 5, 6, 17, 19, 22

Howling 13–14, 18
Hunting 6, 9–11, 13,
    23, 27

Mates 3, 14, 19
Meat 9, 10, 11, 26
Mesocyon 7
Mice 10, 11
Milk 19

Native North
    Americans 7

Origin 7

Packs 2–3, 5–6, 7, 10,
    11, 13, 14, 15, 17,
    19, 21, 22, 23
People 5, 14, 19, 23
Playing 2, 21, 25–27
Population 7
Prey 10, 11, 22
Pups 2–3, 11, 14,
    17–27

Ravens 26, 27

Red wolves 2
Running 9–10, 11, 21,
    25, 26–27

Senses 3, 9, 18, 22
Sight 9, 18
Size 1, 15, 18
Sleeping 2, 6, 7, 19,
    21, 23, 26
Smelling 3, 9, 22
Swimming 3

Talking 13–15, 18, 23,
    25
Teaching 22–23, 27
Territories 5–6, 13, 23
Timber wolves 1, 2
Traveling 2, 6, 23
Tundra 5
Tunnels 17, 19

United States 7

Wagging 15, 18, 25
Weight 1, 18